LIFE CYCLE OF A...

Kangaroo

Revised and Updated

Angela Royston

Heinemann Library
Chicago, Illinois

www.heinemannraintree.com
Visit our website to find out more information about Heinemann-Raintree books.

To order:
☎ Phone 888-454-2279
🖥 Visit www.heinemannraintree.com to browse our catalog and order online.

Edited by Adrian Vigliano, Harriet Milles, and Diyan Leake
Designed by Kimberly R. Miracle and Tony Miracle
Original illustrations ©Capstone Global Library Limited
   1998, 2009
Illustrated by Alan Fraser
Picture research by Tracy Cummins and Heather Mauldin
Originated by Chroma Graphics (Overseas) Pte. Ltd.
Printed in China by South China Printing Company Ltd.

13 12 11 10 09
10 9 8 7 6 5 4 3 2 1

New edition ISBNs: 978 1 4329 2533 8 (hardcover)
                    978 1 4329 2550 5 (paperback)

The Library of Congress has cataloged the first edition as follows:
Royston, Angela.
   Life cycle of a kangaroo / by Angela Royston.
      p. cm.
Includes index.
Summary: An introduction to the life cycle of a kangaroo from its first few months in its mother's pouch until it is four years old.
   ISBN 1-57572-615-7 (lib. Bdg.)
1. Kangaroos—Life cycles—Juvenile literature. [1. Kangaroos.]
I. Title
   QL737.M35R69 1998
   599.2'22—dc21
            97-39696

Acknowledgments
The author and publishers are grateful to the following for permission to reproduce copyright material:
Alamy pp. **11** (©Tim Graham), **12** (©Dave Watts), **25** (©Auscape International Pty Ltd.); Getty Images pp. **10**, **28 bottom** (©Howie Garber), **26** (©Jason Edwards), **14**, **22**, **29 top left**, **29 bottom** (©Natphotos); ©National Geographic pp. **5** (©MINDEN PICTURES/GERRY ELLIS), **16** (©MINDEN PICTURES/NORBERT WU); Nature Focus p. **6** (© A. Young); Peter Arnold Inc. p. **4** (©Biosphoto/Klein J.-L. & Hubert M.-L.), **19** (©FERRERO/LABAT/PHONE); Photolibrary pp. **7**, **28 top left** (©OSF/Alan Root), **9** (©Photodisc), **13** (©Steve Turner), **17** (©OSF/David B. Fleetham), **24** (©Jurgen & Christine Sohns); Photoshot pp. **15** (©NPHA/A N T), **20**, **21** (©NPHA/David Watts); Shutterstock pp. **8**, **28 top right** (©Kitch Bain), **18**, **29 top right** (©Brooke Whatnall), **27** (©Cre8tive Images); Visuals Unlimited p. **23** (©Theo Allofs).

Cover photograph of a kangaroo reproduced with permission of Getty Images (©Robert Harding World Imagery/Thorsten Milse).

Every effort has been made to contact copyright holders of any material reproduced in this book. Any omissions will be rectified in subsequent printings if notice is given to the publisher.

We would like to thank Michael Bright for his invaluable help in the preparation of this book.

Contents

Some words are shown in bold, **like this**. You can find out what they mean by looking in the glossary.

Meet the Kangaroos

This photo shows a gray kangaroo.

Kangaroos are found in Australia and New Guinea. There are 50 different kinds of kangaroos. The kangaroo in this book is a gray kangaroo.

Newborn	5-6 months	6-8 months

Kangaroos are also found in New Guinea. This kangaroo likes to live in trees.

One kind of kangaroo lives in trees. Another kind is as small as a rat! Every kangaroo spends the first few months of its life in its mother's **pouch**.

10-18 months

2 years

4 years

Newborn

A female kangaroo licks her pouch to make it ready for her baby.

A baby kangaroo is called a **joey**. Just before it is born, its mother licks the inside of her **pouch**. The female gives birth after about 40 days.

Newborn

5-6 months

6-8 months

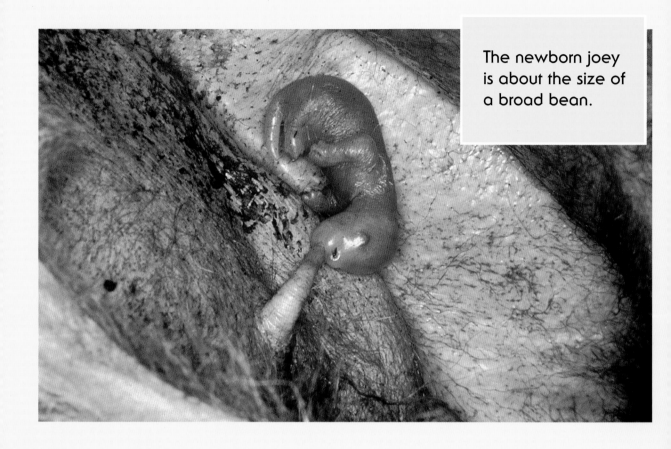

The newborn joey is about the size of a broad bean.

The newborn joey is tiny. He crawls through his mother's fur and into her pouch. There he finds a **teat** and holds on fast with his mouth.

5–6 Months

The **joey** drinks milk from his mother and grows bigger. Sometimes he pops his head out of the **pouch** and looks around.

A female kangaroo is called a doe.

Newborn

5-6 months

6-8 months

At six months old, a joey can eat grass as well as drink milk.

The joey is safe inside the pouch. When his mother feeds, he nibbles some grass. But one day his mother tips him out of the pouch!

10-18 months

2 years

4 years

6–8 Months

At first the **joey** is scared, but he soon starts bouncing around. He loves to **box** and play with his mother.

Kangaroos use their tails to help them stand upright.

Newborn

5-6 months

6-8 months

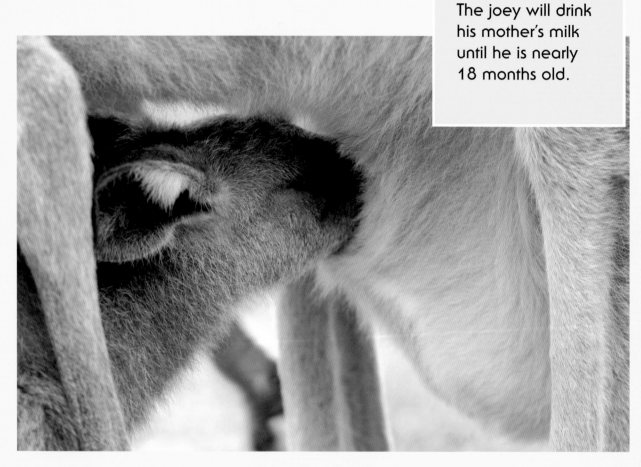

The joey will drink his mother's milk until he is nearly 18 months old.

When he is thirsty, the joey dips his head into his mother's **pouch** for a drink of milk. When he is tired, he climbs back into the pouch.

10-18 months

2 years

4 years

8–10 Months

Eagles like this one can kill animals twice their size.

While the **joey** plays, his mother looks out for danger. This eagle may be looking for a meal. It may attack the joey.

Newborn

5-6 months

6-8 months

Adult kangaroos can keep themselves and their young safe from most other animals.

His mother calls to him. The joey dives headfirst into her **pouch**. He is safe now! He turns around inside the pouch.

10-18 months

2 years

4 years

10–18 Months

Young kangaroos like to **box** and play-fight with each other.

The **joey** is too big to get into the **pouch** now. He plays with the other joeys, but he still drinks his mother's milk.

Newborn

5-6 months

6-8 months

Kangaroos hop instead of walking or running.

The joey likes to stay quite close to his mother. When she bounds away, he hurries after her!

10-18 months

2 years

4 years

18 Months–2 Years

A group of kangaroos is called a troop, or mob.

The kangaroos and **joeys** stay together in a big group. They live in the **bush**. They feed on grass and leaves.

Newborn

5-6 months

6-8 months

It is safer and cooler to rest during the day.

They feed early in the morning or late at night. During the heat of the day, they rest in the shade of the trees.

10-18 months

2 years

4 years

2–3 Years

Big back feet help make kangaroos good hoppers.

The young kangaroo leaves his mother. He is big enough to look after himself now. He bounds over the grass on his strong back legs.

Newborn

5-6 months

6-8 months

An adult kangaroo's tail can be longer than a man's arm.

His long tail helps him to balance as he flies through the air. He joins a group of other young, male kangaroos.

10-18 months

2 years

4 years

4 Years

Male kangaroos are called bucks.

One evening the young kangaroo notices a female. He wants to **mate** with her, but so does another male. The two males begin to fight.

Newborn

5-6 months

6-8 months

They grab each other with their front legs. The young kangaroo leans back on his tail and kicks with both feet.

Mating

The female kangaroo watches as the young male wins the fight. Then he nuzzles her and clucks gently until she is ready to **mate**.

Adult male kangaroos are bigger than females.

Newborn

5-6 months

6-8 months

Forty days after mating, a new **joey** will be born. It will grow inside the female kangaroo's **pouch**.

The female kangaroo will not touch the new joey while it is still tiny.

Living in the Bush

A **pack** of dingoes can surround a kangaroo and attack it.

Dingoes are the kangaroos' enemy. The kangaroos bang their tails on the ground to warn the mob of danger.

Newborn

5-6 months

6-8 months

The kangaroos will move fast to escape enemies.

Now all the kangaroos have smelled the dingoes! They thump the ground with their back legs and bound away.

10-18 months

2 years

4 years

Farmers use barbed wire fences to keep kangaroos off crops.

The **dingo** is not the kangaroo's only enemy. If a kangaroo goes onto farmland, the farmer may shoot it.

Newborn

5-6 months

6-8 months

Kangaroos are the national symbol of Australia.

A kangaroo is safest in the **bush**. There it may live for 15 years, **grazing** with the other kangaroos.

10-18 months

2 years

4 years

Life Cycle

Newborn joey

5–6 months

6–8 months

10–18 months

2–3 years

4 years

Fact File

- A newborn **joey** is about 1 inch (2.5 centimeters) long, not even as long as your little finger.

- A fully grown male gray kangaroo is as tall as a man. Some red kangaroos grow even taller.

- A kangaroo can jump 42 feet (12.8 meters). With one big hop, it could jump over two parked cars.

- A kangaroo can move as fast as a car (up to 40 miles, or 64 kilometers, per hour) to escape from danger.

Glossary

box playful fighting

bush Australian word for open country

dingo type of wild dog found in Australia

grazing animals eating grass

joey name for a young kangaroo from the time it is born until it is old enough to look after itself

mate when a female and a male come together to make babies

pack group of animals

pouch pocket of skin across a female kangaroo's stomach

teat part of a female animal's body where a baby can drink milk

More Books to Read

Niz, Xavier. *World of Mammals: Kangaroos.* Mankato, MN: Capstone Press, 2005.

Ripple, William John, Emily Rose Townsend, and Gail Saunders-Smith. *Desert Animals: Kangaroos.* Pebble Books, 2005.

Spilsbury, Louise and Richard. *Wild World: Watching Kangaroos in Australia.* Chicago: Heinemann Library, 2006.

Index